U.S. Regions

The People of the

Southwest

Blaine Wiseman

MEDIA ENHANCED BOOKS
AV2 BY WEIGL™
ADDED VALUE • AUDIO VISUAL

www.av2books.com

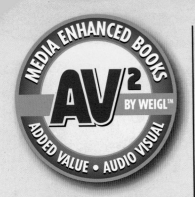

AV² provides enriched content that supplements and complements this book. Weigl's AV² books strive to create inspired learning and engage young minds in a total learning experience.

Your AV² Media Enhanced books come alive with...

Audio
Listen to sections of the book read aloud.

Key Words
Study vocabulary, and complete a matching word activity.

Video
Watch informative video clips.

Quizzes
Test your knowledge.

Embedded Weblinks
Gain additional information for research.

Slide Show
View images and captions, and prepare a presentation.

Try This!
Complete activities and hands-on experiments.

... and much, much more!

Go to **www.av2books.com**, and enter this book's unique code.

BOOK CODE

U445509

AV² by Weigl brings you media enhanced books that support active learning.

Published by AV² by Weigl
350 5th Avenue, 59th Floor
New York, NY 10118

Websites: www.av2books.com   www.weigl.com

Library of Congress Control Number: 2014942101

ISBN 978-1-4896-2466-6 (hardcover)
ISBN 978-1-4896-2467-3 (softcover)
ISBN 978-1-4896-2468-0 (single-user eBook)
ISBN 978-1-4896-2469-7 (multi-user eBook)

Printed in the United States of America in North Mankato, Minnesota
1 2 3 4 5 6 7 8 9 18 17 16 15 14

062014
WEP060614

Project Coordinator: Aaron Carr
Designer: Mandy Christiansen

Every reasonable effort has been made to trace ownership and to obtain permission to reprint copyright material. The publishers would be pleased to have any errors or omissions brought to their attention so that they may be corrected in subsequent printings.

Weigl acknowledges Getty Images as its primary image supplier for this title.

Contents

Introducing the Southwest

The Southwest region is known for its wide open spaces, rugged nature, and strong, hardworking people. Southwesterners live in many different landscapes, such as high mountains, deep canyons, dry deserts, and **fertile** plains. The region has a great deal of natural resources. Southwesterners have used these to build communities, both big and small. From family farms to cities with millions of residents, Southwesterners proudly meet the challenges of the region.

Legend

■	West (11 states)
□	Southwest (5 states)
□	Northeast (11 states)
■	Southeast (11 states)
■	Midwest (12 states)

Where People Live in the Southwest

Compare the populations of the biggest city in each of the Southwestern states.

City	Population
Houston, **Texas**	2,160,821
Denver, **Colorado**	634,265

CANADA

North Dakota

Minnesota

South Dakota

Wisconsin

Lake Superior

Lake Huron

Lake Michigan

Michigan

Lake Ontario

Lake Erie

New Hampshire

Maine

Vermont

Massachusetts

New York

Rhode Island

Connecticut

UNITED STATES

Nebraska

Iowa

Illinois

Indiana

Ohio

Pennsylvania

New Jersey

Delaware

Maryland

Kansas

Missouri

Kentucky

West Virginia

Virginia

Oklahoma

Arkansas

Tennessee

North Carolina

South Carolina

Texas

Mississippi

Alabama

Georgia

Louisiana

Florida

Atlantic Ocean

N

Gulf of Mexico

| 0 | 250 Miles |
| 0 | 250 Kilometers |

City	Population		City	Population
Oklahoma City, **Oklahoma**	599,199		Little Rock, **Arkansas**	196,537
Albuquerque, **New Mexico**	555,417			

*2012 population figures

Settling the Southwest

People have lived in the Southwest for thousands of years. The first residents of the region were ancestors of today's American Indians. They arrived in the region searching for new lands. Ancient peoples hunted herds of large animals and built farming communities throughout the region. American Indian nations such as the Apache, Comanche, Kiowa, Zuni, and many others made this region their home for centuries. While some tribes fought with each other over land and food, they often lived free, peaceful lives.

Traditional life in the Southwest began to change when Europeans arrived. Spanish explorers arrived in the region in the 1500s, followed by the French and British. Most of these explorers were just passing through, but as more people began to arrive, the Southwest was changed forever.

★ In 1830, American Indian groups were forced to move from their homes in the southeast to the west. The Cherokee were one of the last groups to be moved in 1838.

Southwestern Migrations

13,000 BC
The first Americans arrived in Alaska during the Ice Age and moved south looking for a warmer climate. Many settled in the Southwest. One well-known group is the Clovis. Clovis spearpoints have been dated to more than 13,000 years ago.

AD 1821
In 1821, William Becknell traveled west from Missouri to trade in the city of Santa Fe. In 1824, he mapped his route for the U.S. Congress. It became known as the Sante Fe Trail. The trail became an important migration route for about 60 years until the railroad made traveling quicker and easier.

1830
Early in the 1800s, the U.S. government wanted traditional American Indian lands in the east. The Indian Removal Act forced eastern groups to move west of the Mississippi River along the "Trail of Tears." Thousands of Seminole, Creek, Choctaw, Chickasaw, and Cherokee American Indians died along the way.

1862
The Homestead Act allowed anyone over the age of 21 to claim a piece of land in the western territories for free. People rushed to the Southwest, settling on land where they would make their homes. More than 1.6 million people built new lives thanks to the Homestead Act.

1889
In the decades after the Indian Removal Act, settlers rushed to the Southwest. They soon began asking the government for land in the Indian Territory. At noon on April 22, 1889, their wish was granted. Families camped alongside the land. When the clock struck 12:00, they raced into the territory, claiming their new lands. More than 50,000 people took part in the "Oklahoma Land Run" that day.

Historic Events

Many important events in the history of the United States have taken place in the Southwest. The region has played a major role in U.S. exploration and expansion. It has seen war and disaster, and has been the site of major discoveries. All of these historical events, and the people involved, have helped shape the region and the nation.

Mexican–American War (1846–1848)

In 1845, the U.S. government **annexed** Texas. The U.S. and Mexican governments argued about how much area Texas covered. This led to war. In the end, the United States took control of land that makes up California, Nevada, Arizona, Utah, and the Southwestern states of Texas, New Mexico, and Colorado.

Long Walk of the Navajo (1864)

As more settlers arrived in the Southwest, they began settling on Navajo land. This led to conflicts, and in 1864, the government decided to remove the Navajo. Armed soldiers forced 8,500 Navajo to walk more than 300 miles (483 kilometers) through New Mexico. About 200 people died on the 18-day walk.

Spindletop Oil Discovery (1901)

In 1901, the world was searching for new sources of oil to fuel machines and vehicles. After three months of drilling at Spindletop Hill in Texas, oil spurted from 1,020 feet (310 meters) underground. At the time, the well produced more oil than every other well in the United States combined, and created a booming oil industry in Texas.

Oklahoma City Bombing (1995)

On April 19, 1995, a bomb exploded outside a government building in Oklahoma City. The explosion killed 168 people, including 19 small children, and injured about 650 more. At the time, it was the worst terrorist attack in U.S. history. Today, a memorial and museum stand at the site of the bombing.

The Dust Bowl was caused when a drought in the southwest stopped the wheat crops from growing. Strong winds picked up the soil and blew "black blizzards" of dust all over the country.

Stephen F. Austin was one of the leaders of the Texas Revolution. He was known as "The Father of Texas." The state capital, Austin, is named after him.

16,000 people
left Dust Bowl areas, such as Oklahoma, and headed to California in the 1930s. These migrants became known as "Okies."

Historic Southwesterners

The Southwest is home to big things. The biggest mountains in the U.S. and some of the biggest states are found in the Southwest. It is also home to people who make a big difference. Southwestern explorers, pioneers, and leaders have had a big impact on the region, the country, and the world.

Zebulon M. Pike (1779–1813)

Captain Zebulon Montgomery Pike is not a well-known explorer, but he made important discoveries in the Southwest. In 1806 and 1807, he explored much of what is now Colorado. He discovered the source of the Arkansas River and many mountains, including the now famous Pike's Peak.

Sam Houston (1793–1863)

Sam Houston moved to the Southwest in the middle of a successful political career. When the Texas Revolution started, he was made Commander of the Texan Army. He defeated the Mexican Army and became the first president of the Republic of Texas in 1836. After Texas joined the United States, Houston served as a U.S. senator until 1860.

Kit Carson (1809–1868)

As a teenager, Kit Carson left his home in Missouri and followed the Santa Fe Trail. From New Mexico, he traveled the Southwest and West regions, exploring, trapping, and guiding. Carson spent much of his time living with American Indians. He became an enemy of the Navajo, however, by leading the Long Walk in 1864 that forced them from their land.

Quanah Parker (1845–1911)

Quanah Parker was the last chief of the Comanche American Indians. For several years, he led the Comanche in a rebellion against the U.S. government across the plains of Texas. However, his passion for tradition and cooperation with the government made Parker an important **ally** to people from both cultures.

Jack Johnson (1878–1946)

Jack Johnson was born in Galveston, Texas. In 1908, he became the first African American heavyweight boxing champion of the world. He held the title for six years, winning 80 of his 114 matches in his long and successful career. During his career, he experienced racism, which he fought throughout his life.

Howard Hughes (1905–1976)

Howard Hughes was born in Houston, Texas. He took over his family's successful business when he was just 18. Hughes used his fortune to pay for his expensive hobbies. He was a well known movie producer and a famous aviator. During the 1930s and 1940s, Hughes broke air-speed records and made many changes to the way airplanes are built.

Katherine Anne Porter (1890–1980)

One of the United States' most celebrated writer's, Katherine Anne Porter never forgot her roots. Growing up in the Southwest had a major influence on Porter's writings. Some of her most famous stories were based on her experiences in Texas and Colorado. In 1966, Porter won the Pulitzer Prize and the National Book Award for her writing.

Cultural Groups

Throughout history, many different cultures have come together to shape the Southwest. American Indians have lived in each Southwestern state for thousands of years. Today, people of European descent are the majority. The first Europeans in the Southwest were Spanish. Millions of Hispanic people now live in the region, especially in Texas and New Mexico. A large number of communities also reflect the German background of their residents. After slavery was abolished, African Americans gained more influence. There are large African American populations in every state, and there are also large numbers of people with Asian backgrounds in the region.

★ Mariachi is a kind of folk music from Mexico. It is played mostly with string instruments.

Cultural Communities

Across the Southwest, certain neighborhoods reflect the cultural backgrounds of the people who live there.

Sunnyside, Houston, Texas
Sunnyside was formed in 1912 on ranch land around a new school for the area's children. It joined Houston in 1956. About 90 percent of Sunnyside's residents are African American.

Asian District, Oklahoma City, Oklahoma
Oklahoma City's Asian District was built by Vietnamese **refugees** in the 1970s. This colorful area is also known as "Little Saigon." It is well known for its Vietnamese food and shops.

Five Points, Denver, Colorado
Five Points is one of Denver's oldest neighborhoods, well known for its jazz and food scenes. The African American area has been called the "Harlem of the West," after the famous New York neighborhood.

West Side, San Antonio, Texas
San Antonio is the fastest-growing major city in the United States. Of the 1.3 million people in the city, two-thirds are of Hispanic heritage, with more arriving every day. The city's West Side neighborhoods are well-known for their Hispanic culture.

Major Cities of the Southwest

Texas is home to most of the Southwest's big cities, but the other states are home to bustling urban centers, too.

Albuquerque is the largest city in New Mexico. It was built by the Spanish on the site of an ancient American Indian farming community. Today, more than 500,000 people call it home, including a large number of scientists and researchers. Technology and space research are large parts of the city's economy.

Denver, Colorado, is a city known for its high quality-of-life. It is considered one of the best places to live in the United States. The Mile-High City is home to more than half a million people and the head offices of many large companies. It was started by gold prospectors, but has now grown into a modern technology center.

Houston, Texas, is the fourth largest city in the United States, with more than 2.1 million people. Over the last 50 years, it has gone through several periods of **boom** and **bust**. It is the center of the American oil industry, and home to many technology companies. Strong business growth has made Houston a fast-growing **metropolis**.

Born from the Oklahoma Land Run, Oklahoma City is home to almost 600,000 people, and is still growing. A warm, sunny climate, and diverse culture attract people to Oklahoma's state capital. The city's strong economy is important to the wide variety of businesses there.

Little Rock's location makes it an important link between the Southwest and Southeast regions. Several main highways pass through the Arkansas capital, connecting it to major cities such as Oklahoma City, Dallas, and Nashville. This location makes it a great place for businesses. There are plenty of jobs for the city's almost 200,000 residents.

State Capitals

Southwestern state capitals play many important roles to their states, region, country, and the world. They are centers of history, culture, business, and politics. The capital is where politicians and business leaders make important decisions that have major impacts on everyone in their state.

State Capitals	Population
Austin, **Texas**	842,592
Denver, **Colorado**	634,265
Oklahoma City, **Oklahoma**	599,199
Little Rock, **Arkansas**	196,537
Santa Fe, **New Mexico**	69,204

*2012 population figures

Little Rock is named for a small group of rocks discovered by a French explorer. Pieces of *Le Petit Rocher*, which means "little rock," can still be seen in the city today.

Denver began as three separate towns. When they came together as one, an argument broke out over which name to use. People from Denver offered to share a barrel of whiskey with the other towns, and they agreed to name the city Denver.

Industries of the Southwest

The diversity of resources found in the Southwest make it a great place for businesses. Abundant natural resources and wide open spaces make it a great location for mining and farming, and other related industries. As more people and businesses move to the region, the economy grows stronger.

Texas

Texas is the second biggest agricultural producer, and the top beef producer in the United States. It produces about 20 percent of the nation's beef. There are more than 13.8 million cattle in Texas, the most in the country.

- **$7.4 billion per year** for sale of cattle
- **14 percent of Texans** are employed in agriculture.

Colorado

Colorado's natural beauty makes it one of the top states in the United States for tourism. Ski resorts, national parks, and other Rocky Mountain attractions are the most important parts of this industry.

- **144,300 people** working in Colorado's tourism industry
- **$15.9 billion**—state earnings from tourism in 2011

Arkansas

Arkansas is one of the country's top two producers of broilers. The state produces 5.7 billion pounds (2.6 billion kilograms) of these young chickens every year.

- **42,000 poultry workers** in Arkansas
- **Contributed $3.7 billion** to state economy in 2012

New Mexico

Mining makes up a large part of New Mexico's economy. Coal, copper, and potash are some of the main minerals mined in the state. Gold and silver are also produced as part of the copper mining process.

- **5,658 mining jobs**
- **$41.2 million** generated from mining in 2012

Oklahoma

Oil and gas are Oklahoma's most important economic resources. The state is among the top five producers of these energy sources in the country.

- **344,503 Oklahomans employed** in oil and gas
- **Generates $52 billion** per year for the state

Southwestern Tourism

Millions of tourists from around the United States and the world travel to the Southwest every year. They are attracted by the beautiful natural areas and famous historic landmarks throughout the region.

Texas

The number one tourist attraction in Texas was originally a Spanish **mission**. Here, in 1836, thousands of Mexican troops attacked a small group of Texans in what is known as the Battle of the Alamo. This battle was part of the Texas Revolution. Today, more than 2.5 million people visit the Alamo every year.

Colorado

Rocky Mountain National Park attracts more than 3 million people each year. They come from all over the world to enjoy the park's natural beauty. Tourists can explore the park's 359 miles (578 km) of hiking trails and 260 miles (418 km) of horse trails. There are more than 700 campsites in the park.

Oklahoma

Known as "America's Main Street," Route 66 is probably the country's most famous highway. It stretches from Chicago to Los Angeles, with the longest section passing through Oklahoma. More than 400 miles (644 km) of this famous road stretch through Tulsa, Oklahoma City, and many other towns. Museums, diners, and attractions such as the 80-foot (24-meter) long concrete Blue Whale are found on Route 66.

Arkansas

Covering 5,550 acres (184 hectares), Hot Springs National Park is the smallest in the United States. The park is also unique because it is located right next to a city. The natural springs are protected, but tourists can soothe their sore muscles in spas that pump the 143° Fahrenheit (61° Celsius) water into town. More than 1 million people visit the park every year.

New Mexico

At least 117 of the world's oldest caves are hidden beneath the Chihuahuan Desert. Carlsbad Caverns have been formed over 20 million years by acid and water carving the rocks of the Guadalupe Mountains. Every year, 300,000 people visit Carlsbad Caverns National Park.

Every day, 700,000 gallons (2.6 million liters) of water flow from the rocks at Hot Springs National Park. This is enough water to fill an Olympic swimming pool.

Fewer than 200 Texans, including the famous Davy Crockett, fought in the Battle of the Alamo. They held off the Mexican attack for 13 days before they were finally defeated.

Famous Southwesterners

Many of the Southwest's most famous people have found inspiration from their region. It has produced some of the world's most well-known artists and entertainers.

Maria Tallchief was born in Fairfax, Oklahoma, in 1925. She died in 2013. A member of the Osage tribe, she was the first American Indian ballerina. Tallchief was one of the world's most famous ballerinas between the 1940s and the 1960s. In 1996, she was **inducted** into the National Women's Hall of Fame. In 1999, she was awarded the National Medal of Arts, the highest award given to artists by the U.S. government.

Born in Tulsa in 1962, **Garth Brooks** began performing while he was studying at Oklahoma State University. He became famous for his rock 'n' roll inspired country music, and his amazing live concerts. One of the most successful country musicians in history, Brooks has sold more than 100 million albums.

Ron Howard was born in Duncan, Oklahoma, in 1954. His acting career began early when his parents, who were both actors, got their baby a movie role at just 18 months of age. He became famous in the 1960s and 1970s for his roles in *The Andy Griffith Show* and *Happy Days*. Later, Howard moved to the other side of the camera, directing films such as *Willow*, *Apollo 13*, and *Parenthood*.

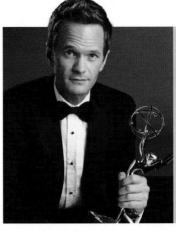

Neil Patrick Harris was born in 1973 in Albuquerque. He started acting in school plays in the town of Ruidoso. When he was 15, Harris got the lead role in the TV show *Doogie Howser M.D.* He became a teenage star playing a teenage surgeon. In the years since then, he has had many other acting jobs, and has won three Emmy Awards.

Brad Pitt was born in Shawnee, Oklahoma, in 1963. He studied journalism at university, but moved to California to become an actor. Pitt's first roles were on daytime soap operas, but he soon became a huge movie star. His acting in movies such as *Legends of the Fall* and *The Curious Case of Benjamin Button* has made him one of Hollywood's biggest stars.

Beyoncé Knowles is known as one of the most successful musicians in the world today. She was born in Houston in 1981 and reached the top of the charts with her group, Destiny's Child, as a teenager. In 2003, Beyoncé left the group to become a solo artist. She has 17 Grammy Awards, and has sold more than 118 million albums.

Dr. Maya Angelou was born in 1928, and moved to Stamps, Arkansas, as a child. She was one of the world's most celebrated writers. She was also a civil rights activist, educator, film producer, singer, and actress. She worked with Civil Rights leaders such as Malcolm X and Dr. Martin Luther King, Jr. In 1970, her first book, *I Know Why the Caged Bird Sings*, became an international bestseller. She has won many awards and more than 50 **honorary** university degrees. Dr. Angelou died in May 2014.

Carrie Underwood was busy studying at university when she became an "American Idol." Born in 1983, and raised on a farm in Muskogee, Oklahoma, Underwood's childhood gave her plenty of songwriting material. In 2004, she won a TV singing contest, and her career took off. Since then, she has sold millions of albums, won dozens of awards, and become one of country music's biggest stars.

Southwestern Politics

For centuries, the Southwest has been driven by politics. Many of America's most well-known leaders have come from the region. While there are many supporters of both major parties in the Southwest, the Republican Party dominates.

Dwight D. Eisenhower grew up in Abilene, Texas, where he was a star football player. He joined the U.S. military, and rose to the highest rank in World War II, Commander of the Allied Forces. A few years after the war, General Eisenhower became President Eisenhower. As president, he worked to end the **Cold War**.

Lyndon B. Johnson was born in Stonewall, Texas. He served as vice president under John F. Kennedy. When Kennedy was **assassinated**, Johnson became president. He served the end of Kennedy's term and was elected to another in 1964. During his presidency, Johnson signed the Civil Rights Act. He also sent more than 500,000 U.S. troops to fight in the Vietnam War.

The Bush family of Texas has produced many governors, and two U.S. presidents. George H. W. Bush (above) served as president for one term from 1989 to 1993. He led the United States through the end of the Cold War and the Gulf War. His son George W. Bush served two terms as president, from 2001 to 2009. After the September 11, 2001 attacks on the U.S., he led the nation into wars in Iraq and Afghanistan.

Hope, Arkansas, is the birthplace of Bill Clinton. He took over the presidency from George H. W. Bush. His two terms, from 1993 to 2001, are remembered as strong economic times. One of Clinton's hobbies is playing the saxophone. Before becoming a politician, he wanted to be a professional musician.

State Politics

Southwestern states supported both parties in the 2012 Presidential election. In the two blue states, a majority of voters supported the Democrats, while red states voted for the Republicans.

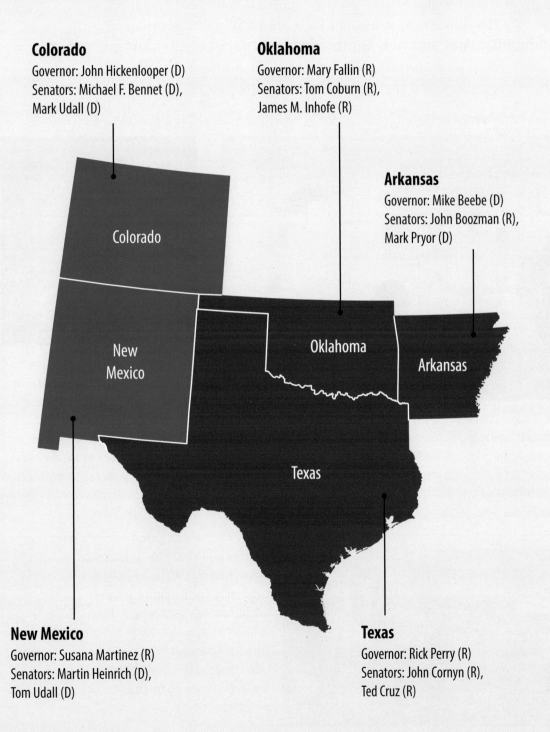

Colorado

Governor: John Hickenlooper (D)
Senators: Michael F. Bennet (D),
Mark Udall (D)

Oklahoma

Governor: Mary Fallin (R)
Senators: Tom Coburn (R),
James M. Inhofe (R)

Arkansas

Governor: Mike Beebe (D)
Senators: John Boozman (R),
Mark Pryor (D)

New Mexico

Governor: Susana Martinez (R)
Senators: Martin Heinrich (D),
Tom Udall (D)

Texas

Governor: Rick Perry (R)
Senators: John Cornyn (R),
Ted Cruz (R)

Monuments and Buildings

With so much history in the region, it is no surprise that the Southwest is home to a wide variety of historical landmarks. For centuries, Southwesterners have been building homes, forts, and monuments, leaving their mark on the region. These places help tell the story of the region's people.

The Alamo was founded around 1718 by Spanish settlers who called it *Mission San Antonio de Valero*. In the 1800s, the mission complex became home to Spanish soldiers. They renamed it "El Alamo," which means, "The Cottonwood," because it was surrounded by cottonwood trees. Texans took over the complex during the Texas Revolution. A few months later, Texas became its own nation.

Petroglyph National Monument is a 7,244 acre (2,420 ha) area that is home to almost 20,000 historic rock carvings. Over centuries, Puebloan American Indians and Spanish settlers carved pictures into the ancient volcanic rocks in the area. The carvings show what life was like in the New Mexican desert between 400 and 700 years ago.

For more than 1,000 years, Taos American Indians have lived in the same New Mexico community. Taos Pueblo is a group of **adobe** buildings that have been home to the same group since before Europeans arrived in America. It is considered the oldest community still **inhabited** in the United States. Today, it is a protected landmark.

From the year AD 450, the Puebloan people lived in what is now Mesa Verde National Park. These ancestors of modern American Indians built communities among the canyons and cliffs of southwestern Colorado. While the people disappeared around 800 years ago, their homes and communities are still standing.

Reaching 4,226 feet (1,288 m) across the Arkansas River, Big Dam Bridge is the world's longest pedestrian and cycle bridge. The bridge is part of a dam that cuts across the river, creating Murray Lake. Unlike other dam bridges, this one is built into the dam, rather than on top. It is the only bridge of its kind in the world.

The San Jacinto Monument is the world's tallest war memorial. It stands 567 feet (173 m) above the battlefield where Texas gained its independence. At the base of the monument, a museum and carvings tell the history of Texas and its fight for nationhood. Construction was completed in 1939 after three years of work. From the observation floor, visitors can look out at the historic battlefield and the city of Houston.

Flags and Seals

State flags and seals feature the symbols that make each state unique. A state flies its flag above buildings, monuments, parks, and other important properties. Seals are another official way of claiming ownership, usually of an item or a document.

Colorado

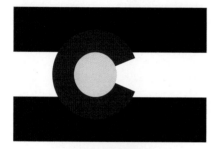

New Mexico

Flag The white on the flag represents snow on the mountains, and the blue indicates the clear blue skies of Colorado. Red, white, and blue matches the colors on the U.S. flag.

Seal The **fasces** on this seal stands for strength and leadership. The mountains show the natural beauty of the state, and 1876 is the year Colorado became a state.

Flag Red and yellow are the colors of Spain. These colors represent the large Spanish population in New Mexico. The four groups of four lines show the following: four points of the compass (North, East, South, West), four seasons (spring, summer, fall, winter), four parts of the day (morning, noon, evening, night), and four seasons of life (childhood, youth, adulthood, old age).

Seal The Mexican eagle with a snake in its beak and cactus in its talons are symbols of an ancient Aztec myth showing the state's pride for its Mexican heritage. New Mexico became a state in 1912.

Arkansas

Flag The Arkansas flag is red, white, and blue—the colors of the United States. The diamond shape shows that Arkansas is the only state that produces diamonds. There are 25 white stars, showing that Arkansas was the 25th state to join the United States.

Seal The main feature of this seal is the eagle with a scroll in its beak, and arrows and an olive branch in its talons. These represent power and peace. The sword stands for justice.

Oklahoma

Flag Blue stands for the sky, and the rawhide shield and eagle feathers represent the American Indian warriors of the state.

Seal Inside the star, there are six scenes. In the middle, an American Indian is shaking hands with a settler, symbolizing cooperation. Each point on the star symbolizes one of the five American Indian nations in the territory— the Chickasaw, the Cherokee, the Creek, the Seminole, and the Choctaw.

Texas

Flag The Texan flag is very simple. Red stands for bravery, white for purity, blue for loyalty, and the Lone Star for independence.

Seal The Lone Star is also featured on the front of the seal, along with an oak branch that stands for strength and an olive branch for peace. The main features on the back of the seal are the Alamo; a cannon representing the Battle of Gonzales; and Vince's Bridge, the destruction of which contributed to the end of the Texas Revolution.

Challenges Facing the Southwest

Drying Up

Much of the Southwest is naturally dry. The Rocky Mountains cause a **rain shadow** over the plains below. Colorado, New Mexico, and Texas have large desert areas. There are several major rivers, but very few natural lakes. These factors make water management the most important long-term issue for the people of the Southwest. Scientists worry that water in the region could run dry within the next 100 years.

Industries such as agriculture are the biggest water users in the Southwest. Farmers use it to **irrigate** their crops. Ranchers need it for their livestock. Other industries such as oil and gas, and mining use huge amounts of water as well. As more people move to the Southwest, and industries grow stronger, more water is used. It is important for industries to use water responsibly. If the water runs dry, there will be none for industry and none to drink.

★ With a population of 5.95 million in 2010, Houston is the sixth largest metro area in the United States.

Spreading Out

The biggest cities in the United States usually have millions of people living close together. Southwestern cities are different. Places such as Houston, Dallas, and Oklahoma City are home to millions of people spread over large areas. With so much land available, people in these cities have preferred to build out, rather than up. This has caused **urban sprawl** unlike anywhere else in the country.

★ Instead of living in highrise apartment buildings, most people in Southwestern cities live in suburban houses.

Urban sprawl causes many problems for the environment. In sprawling cities, more people have to drive cars instead of using public transport. As a city spreads, it destroys natural areas. Houston has even been called "the blob that ate East Texas." While these cities continue growing, some people are trying to stop the problem. City planners are developing more dense urban areas and better public transport to bring people closer together.

In 2013, an agency in Texas wanted to buy Red River water from Oklahoma. When Oklahoma refused to sell it, the Texas agency sued. Oklahoma won the Supreme Court case and got to keep its water.

Houston is the most sprawling city in the U.S. It covers **600 square miles** (1,554 square kilometers).

Quiz

1 Which American Indian groups were moved by the *Indian Removal Act*?

2 Which city is home to an area called "Little Saigon?"

3 Who was the first American Indian ballerina?

4 Which father and son from Texas have both served as U.S. president?

5 Who was the first African American heavyweight boxing champion of the world?

6 Which is the largest city in the Southwest?

7 What is the oldest community still inhabited in the United States?

8 Which state is a major producer of young chickens, called broilers?

9 What road is known as "America's Main Street?"

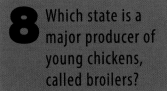

10 Which Southwestern state joined the Union in 1876?

ANSWERS: 1. Choctaw, Chickasaw, Creek, Cherokee, and Seminole **2.** Oklahoma City **3.** Maria Tallchief **4.** George H.W. Bush and George W. Bush **5.** Jack Johnson **6.** Houston, Texas **7.** Taos Pueblo, New Mexico **8.** Arkansas **9.** Route 66 **10.** Colorado

Key Words

adobe: a mixture of water, earth, and straw used for building

annexed: took the territory for themselves

assassinated: murdered for political reasons

boom: a time of economic growth

bust: a time of economic decline

Cold War: a conflict that caused tension between the United States and the then Soviet Union between 1945 and 1989–1991

fasces: a bundle of rods wrapped around an axe, tied with ribbon

fertile: good conditions for growing plants

honorary: given to someone as an honor in recognition of excellence in their area of knowledge, such as a university degree

inducted: to be formally recognized and admitted to a group or society

inhabited: lived in

irrigate: taking water from one place to another to grow crops or plants

metropolis: a large city

mission: a place where people spread their religion or beliefs in a new area

rain shadow: an area where little rain falls because clouds cannot get passed the tall mountains

refugees: people who have been forced to leave their home by war or other disaster

urban sprawl: the term used to describe a city that is spread out over a large area

Index

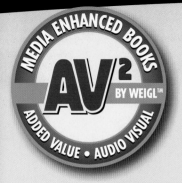

Log on to www.av2books.com

AV² by Weigl brings you media enhanced books that support active learning. Go to www.av2books.com, and enter the special code found on page 2 of this book. You will gain access to enriched and enhanced content that supplements and complements this book. Content includes video, audio, weblinks, quizzes, a slide show, and activities.

AV² Online Navigation

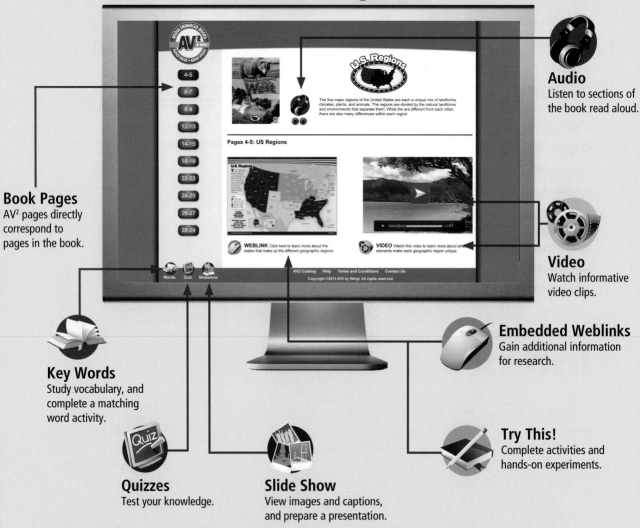

Book Pages
AV² pages directly correspond to pages in the book.

Key Words
Study vocabulary, and complete a matching word activity.

Quizzes
Test your knowledge.

Slide Show
View images and captions, and prepare a presentation.

Audio
Listen to sections of the book read aloud.

Video
Watch informative video clips.

Embedded Weblinks
Gain additional information for research.

Try This!
Complete activities and hands-on experiments.

AV² was built to bridge the gap between print and digital. We encourage you to tell us what you like and what you want to see in the future.

Sign up to be an AV² Ambassador at www.av2books.com/ambassador.